TABLE OF CONTENTS

CHAPTER 1

ON TOP OF THE WORLD

Who is Odin? What does he do? How does he die?

Odin was a Norse god. **Norse** means from the Norway area. Norse people were **Vikings**. Vikings traveled by sea. They raided. They attacked. They were warriors. They believed in many gods.

Odin's name means "master of fury." He was a creator god. He was the father of all gods. He was the father of all humans. He was called "All father."

Frost giants ruled the world. Ymir was the leader of the giants. Odin and his brothers killed the giants. They used Ymir's body to make the universe. They made the heavens for the gods. He and his brothers made the earth for humans. They made the **underworld** for the dead. The underworld is where dead people go. They made the first humans from trees.

Odin ruled **Asgard**. It was the universe's center. It was where the Aesir gods lived. There were two tribes of Norse gods and goddesses. They were the Aesir and the Vanir.

Aesir is Odin's tribe of Norse gods.

Odin had many children.

Odin was the most powerful god. He lived in Valaskjalf. This was the name of his house. It means "shelf of the dead." It had a tall tower. His throne was at the top. His throne was called Hlidskjalf. He sat there. He saw over all the worlds. He saw everything. He also lived in **Valhalla**. This means "hall of the dead."

Odin married Frigg. Frigg was the goddess of marriage. They had sons. Odin went to the land of giants. He fell in love with Jord. Jord was the goddess of earth. They had a son. His name was Thor. Thor was Odin's most famous child.

Odin fought in **Ragnarok**. This was the final battle. It was the end of the world. It was known as the "doom of the gods."

Family Tree

Grandparents: Buri (first god), Bolthorn (frost giant)

Parents: Borr (god of mountains) and Bestla (god of water and ice)

Brothers: Vili (god of motivation) and Ve (god of holy shrines)

Spouse: Frigg (wife, goddess of marriage) and Jord (lover, giant, goddess of earth)

Children: Baldur (god of love and light), Hod (god of winter and darkness, often called Hodr), Hermod (messenger of the gods), Thor (god of thunder), Vali (born to avenge his brother Baldur's death), and Vidar (god of revenge), Heimdall (guardian of the gods, mothers were the Nine Waves)

Odin was killed by Fenrir. Fenrir was a giant wolf. The gods made him. They raised him. They thought they could control him. He kept growing. He broke his chains. At Ragnarok, Fenrir broke free. He ran around the world. His lower jaw was on the ground. His upper jaw was in the sky. He ate everything in his way.

Odin had a son with another female giant. His name was Vidar. Vidar was the god of revenge. He killed Fenrir. He ripped apart his jaws.

Fenrir broke his chains with a single shake.

CHAPTER 2

WORLD TRAVELER

How does Odin help humans? What are his powers?

Odin was the god of poetry. He stole poetry from the giants. He only spoke in poems. He spoke in phrases. He spoke in riddles. He had a soft voice. He gave poetry as a gift. He loved beautiful words. Poets worshiped him.

Odin was the god of wisdom. He was the god of learning. He liked to help humans. He gave them knowledge. He went on long walks. He went by himself. He learned things. He shared what he learned. He made people smart. He made people happy. But he also made people mean. He was also the god of war.

Odin traveled to all the worlds. He took the shape of an old man. He was tall. He had a long beard. He wore a blue coat. He was strong. He had muscles. He had one eye. His eye was bright. It was like the sun. Odin wore a floppy hat. He covered his missing eye.

Odin guided warriors and poets.

All in the Family

Hod was Odin's son. He's blind. He's known for one thing. He killed his twin brother, Baldur. Everyone loved Baldur. Baldur had dreams of dying. His mother was Frigg. She was worried. She made everyone promise not to hurt Baldur. Loki is another god. He liked playing tricks. He made a mistletoe dart. Gods threw darts at Baldur. Darts fell off him. Loki told Hod to throw the mistletoe dart at Baldur. Hod did it. He killed Baldur. Everyone was sad. This created winter. Odin had a son with a female giant. The son's name was Vali. Vali grew up in one day. His job was to kill Hod. He shot Hod with an arrow.

Odin could change into other shapes. He could be any animal.

He was the god of magic. He healed. He saw people's futures. He saw their pasts. He traveled in people's memories. He traveled in people's dreams.

He was a strong leader. He ruled by magic and wit. He liked being smart. He liked being creative. He helped **outlaws**. Outlaws are rebels. They break laws.

CHAPTER 3

LORD OF WAR

What does Odin do as the god of war? What happens at Valhalla?

Odin was the god of war. He liked to start wars. He liked to pit humans against each other. He liked violence. He liked blood. He liked **chaos**. Chaos means disorder. Odin liked warriors who fought like wolves or bears. He was the master of these animals.

Odin decided who won wars. So, humans worshipped him. They did this during wartime. They made **sacrifices**. Sacrifice means giving up something to get something. Humans gave up their lives. They promised to honor Odin.

They asked for good luck. They asked for special skills. They asked for tips. They begged to win.

Odin showed up in battle. He had many skills. He made his enemies blind. He made them deaf. He made them sick. Sometimes he made their weapons hit like sticks. He made his warriors go **berserk**. Berserk means crazy.

Odin tricked people into fighting each other. He was sly.

Real World Connection

There's a dog named Odin. Odin is a K9 officer. This means he's a police dog. He's trained to help cops. He lives in Texas. His partner is Deputy Andrew Blauser. Blauser handles him. He takes care of Odin. Damon Allen was a cop. He was shot. This happened at a traffic stop. It happened on Thanksgiving Day. The shooter was Dabrett Black. He ran away. Many people searched for him. They searched for 5 hours. No one could find him. But Odin did. He bit Black. He took him down. Odin was honored. He became "Employee of the Year." The sheriff's office said, "Great job to K9 Odin and his partner Deputy Blauser."

Odin was known to lead the army of the dead.

Odin liked strong warriors. He valued courage. He valued bravery. Warriors wanted to win Odin's favor. They threw spears at their enemies. They shouted, "Odin owns ye all!"

Odin talked to the dead. He made them speak. He questioned them. He wanted to learn what they knew.

Odin ruled the **Valkyries**. They were female spirits. They were warrior women. They flew over battlefields. They watched over warriors dying in battle. They took the strong warriors. They took the war heroes. They took half of them to Valhalla. Valhalla is where the souls of warriors went. The other half went to Freya. Freya was the goddess of love, war, and death.

Dead warriors wanted to go to Valhalla. They thought it was an honor. Odin fed them. He gave them a big party. He trained them. He built his army for Ragnarok.

Odin was the protector of war heroes.

CHAPTER 4

ODIN'S BUDDIES

What are Odin's weapons? What are Odin's animal companions?

Odin carried a spear. The spear was magical. It was made from a magical tree. **Dwarfs** made it. Dwarfs were special creatures. They had magic. Odin wrote magical letters on it. The spear was named Gungnir. This means "swaying one." It always hit its mark. It never missed.

Odin had a magical ring. The ring was gold. It was called Draupnir. This means "the dripper." It was also made by dwarfs. Eight new rings dropped out of it. This happened every ninth day. All the rings were gold. This made Odin rich.

Gungnir and Draupnir were gifts to the gods. (Another gift was Thor's hammer.)

Draupnir represents fertility.

Animal companions are called familiars.

Sleipnir was a magical horse. He had eight legs. He flew. He ran on land. He ran on water. He was fast. He was gray. He was the most beautiful horse. He had magical letters on his teeth. Odin rode him. Sleipnir was like the wind. He could ride in and out of the underworld. His father was Loki. Loki was the god of fire. He liked to play tricks. He gave Sleipnir to Odin.

Odin had two wolves. The wolves were named Geri and Freki. Their names mean "the **ravenous** and greedy one." Ravenous means really hungry. They followed Odin everywhere. Odin gave them his food. He only drank wine.

Cross-Cultural Connection

Varuna was an Indian god. He's like Odin. He was the god of sky. He was the god of waters. He was the god of justice. He was the god of truth. He was one of the first gods. He was the supreme lord of the world. He had a thousand eyes. He saw everything. He kept order. He kept everything working. He moved the sun in the sky. He separated the day and night. He was everywhere. He knew all thoughts. He wore golden armor. He rode Makara. Makara was a sea monster. Varuna's weapon was a pasha. A pasha is a snake. It became a rope with a loop. Varuna punished humans. He caught them with a pasha.

Huginn and Muninn were magical birds. They were ravens. Huginn represented thought. Muninn represented memory. Odin gave them the gift of speech. He sent them out every morning. The ravens helped Odin. They traveled far and wide. They traveled all over the worlds. They came back at night. They whispered into Odin's ear. They brought news to him. They told him what they saw. They told him what they heard. They reported everything. Odin loved them. He worried they wouldn't return. When not traveling, they were with Odin. They sat on his shoulders.

Odin was known as the raven god.

CHAPTER 5

IN SEARCH OF WISDOM

What are some stories about Odin? How does he gain wisdom?

Mimir was Odin's uncle. He was the wisest god. He advised the gods. He guarded the Well of Knowledge. This was a magical well. Anyone who drank from it gained wisdom. Odin wanted knowledge. He made a deal with Mimir. He gave him his eye. He did this to get a sip from the well. This made Odin smart. He gained Mimir's wisdom.

There was a war. Mimir was killed. Odin took Mimir's head. He put it in magical herbs. He said some magical words. He carried around the head. Mimir's head helped Odin. It advised him. It told him secrets.

Mimir's well came from the roots of Yggdrasil. This was a magical tree. It had great wisdom. It was called the "tree of life." It was also called "world tree."

Odin stabbed himself with Gungnir. He didn't eat. He was in pain. He sacrificed himself. He died, but came back to life.

Mimir means "the wise one."

He gained knowledge of the **runes**. Runes are symbols. They're secrets. They're like letters. They're used for writing. They're used to tell fortunes.

Explained By Science

Like Odin, many people have one eye. They may have a sick eye. Doctors remove it. Enucleation is the name of the surgery. People learn to see with one eye. Their field of vision is smaller. This means they can't see as much. They lose about 20 percent of what they see from the sides. They may bump into things more. They also can't judge distances as well. They can't figure out the depth of things within 3 feet (1 meter) of them. They can't tell how far apart things are. They have a hard time driving. They have a hard time playing sports. They have a hard time shaking hands. They have a hard time pouring drinks. People's brains will learn to focus. They take over the work of the missing eye.

Winds shook the tree of life.

Odin died again in Ragnarok. This time he didn't come back to life. Fenrir crushed him.

Don't anger the gods. Odin had great powers. And he knew how to use them.

DID YOU KNOW?

- Odin is known by over 200 names. He's the god with the most names.
- "Wednesday" is named after Odin. It comes from "Wodensdag" or "Onsday." This means "Odin's Day."
- There's a great temple in Sweden. It has statues of Thor, Odin, and Freya. Vikings made human sacrifices. They prayed to Thor for good weather for their crops. They prayed to Odin in times of war. They prayed to Freya for weddings.
- Odin created the first humans. He gave them soul and life. The humans were named Ask and Embla. Odin's brother Vili gave them wit. Odin's other brother, Ve, gave them senses.
- Odin is the leader of the Wild Hunt. This is an army of the dead. They march across the winter sky.
- Odin was a bit of a snob. He liked rulers and rich people.
- Odin became too much at times. Humans got mad at Odin. The gods of Asgard banned Odin for 10 years. They didn't want to be connected with Odin. They wanted to win back humans' favor.
- Baldur was Odin's son. He died. Odin placed Draupnir on Baldur's funeral fire.
- Odin and his brothers used Ymir to make the world. They used his flesh to make the earth. They used his skull to make the sky. They used his bones to make the mountains. They used his blood to make the seas.
- Some humans sacrificed themselves for Odin. They hung themselves from a tree. They stabbed themselves with spears. They did this to be like Odin at Yggdrasil.

CONSIDER THIS!

TAKE A POSITION! Read the 45th Parallel Press book about Thor. Compare Odin and Thor. Odin is supposed to be the "All father." But he's not as popular as Thor. Who is more important: Odin or Thor? Argue your point with reasons and evidence.

SAY WHAT? Read the 45th Parallel Press book about Zeus. Explain how they are the same. Explain how they are different. Which god do you like more?

THINK ABOUT IT! Odin was the god of war. But he was also the god of poetry and wisdom. How does this make sense?

LEARN MORE

Crossley-Holland, Kevin, and Jeffrey Alan Love (illustr.). *Norse Myths: Tales of Odin, Thor and Loki.* Somerville, MA: Candlewick Studio, 2017.

Long, Steven. *Odin: The Viking Allfather.* Oxford: Osprey Publishing, 2015.

Napoli, Donna Jo, and Christina Balit (illust.). *Treasury of Norse Mythology: Stories of Intrigue, Trickery, Love, and Revenge.* Washington, DC: National Geographic, 2015.

GLOSSARY

Asgard (AHS-gahrd) center of the universe where the Aesir gods lived

berserk (bur-ZURK) going crazy

chaos (KAY-ahs) disorder, frenzy

dwarfs (DWORFZ) magical creatures who mine and make magical weapons

Norse (NORS) coming from the Norway area

outlaws (OUT-lawz) rebels, people who break the laws

Ragnarok (RAHG-nuh-rok) the final battle of the gods' world, marking the end of their world

ravenous (RAV-uh-nuhs) really hungry

runes (ROONZ) letters of an ancient language used to write, tell fortunes, or reveal secrets

sacrifices (SAK-ruh-fahys-ez) the giving up of things to get something

underworld (UHN-dur-wurld) the place where the souls of dead people go after they die

Valhalla (val-HAL-uh) hall of the dead where killed warriors are welcomed

Valkyries (val-KEER-eez) female warrior spirits who fly over battlefields and take fallen war heroes to Valhalla

Vikings (VYE-kingz) seafaring warriors who raided and attacked towns

INDEX